# LEARNING ABOUT
# MY PROPHET

The Presidency of Religious Affairs
Publications: 639
Children's books: 160

**Learning About My Prophet**
This book has been written by a group of teachers

**Coordinator**
Dr. Ömer Menekşe

**Pictures**
Osman Turhan

**Press editor**
Mehmet Erdoğan

**Visual editor**
Nurullah Özbay

**Translator**
Irfan DURAN

**Redaction**
Ayşe Zuhal Sarı
Ahmet Kahraman

**Graphic-Design**
Mücella Tekin

**ANKARA • 2017**

**3rd Edition**

**High Board of Religious Affairs Decision**
07.04.2005/66

**2017-06-Y-0003-639**
ISBN 978-975-19-3707-0

**Press**
Epa-Mat Bas. Yay. Prom. San. ve
Tic. Ltd. Şti.
+90 312 394 48 63

**Contact**
Üniversiteler Mah. Dumlupınar Bulv.
No : 147/A 06800 Çankaya/Ankara
Tel.: +90 312 295 72 81
Fax: +90 312 284 72 88
www.diyanet.gov.tr
yabancidiller@diyanet.gov.tr

# FOREWORD

Hi Kids,

Learning and loving our Prophet is the best source of happiness. His life is full of good examples for us. In this book, you will find our Prophet Muhammad's leading life and his struggle to explain Islam to people.

First of all, our Prophet was a father. He would love his children and would pay attention to them. He would respect his wife and he was helpful. His friends would always trust him in any matter.

He would call the humanity to prettiness, honesty, being wise and ethical and helping the people in need.

He wanted the humans to stay away from lying, stealing, killing other people, drinking alcohol, gambling and polluting the environment.

Our Prophet bare many difficult situations for the humans to be in welfare. He suffered hunger and thirst; he was stoned, exiled, wounded in wars but never gave up from his struggle. Because he was sent by Allah to tell the straight path Islam to people.

Dear kids;

Our religion is Islam, our prophet is Muhammad and our holy book is the Qur'an. Once we believe in Allah, love our Prophet and accomplish our holy book's orders, then we will be happy and successful.

Then, we must know our Prophet well, love him, and take him as a model. This book has been prepared to help you in these matters. We hope you will enjoy this book.

You kids are our future and we love you so much…

**THE PRESIDENCY OF RELIGIOUS AFFAIRS**

# LEARNING ABOUT MY PROPHET

PUBLICATIONS OF THE PRESIDENCY OF RELIGIOUS AFFAIRS

# Contents

# PART 1
# THE ORPHAN MUHAMMAD (SAW)

## Everybody was Waiting for Him

The period prior to the emergence of Islam is known as the Jahiliyyah – The Age of Ignorance. In that period, people were uncivilised. The weak and helpless were forced into slavery and cast out from society. The bonds between kin and neighbours were not strong, and people had no trust for each other. Women were debased and newly born girls were buried alive. People worshipped idols and believed in superstitions. Two people who lived during that time explained the following:

"We had ignorant and barbaric lives. We worshipped idols, we were immoral and we fought amongst our kin. We did not respect our neighbors and the strong amongst us oppressed the weak."

"We are the people who lived the Age of Ignorance. We would worship idols and bury our own children alive. I had a daughter. When I called her, she would come running in joy. One day I called her as usual and took her to a nearby well. I grabbed her by the hands and threw her into the well. She cried , 'Father!' Her voice still haunts me."

Was this all that occurred? Definitely not!

People worshipped idols in place of Allah. The house of Allah, the Ka'bah, was filled with idols.

People were forced into slavery and were bought and sold in slave markets. Human life had no value.

The strong oppressed the weak. The weak had nowhere to go in order to seek their rights. The evil were not punished justly.

People would consume vast amounts of alcohol, prostitute women and would gamble all night.

Some individuals were uncomfortable with this situation yet, there was nothing much they could do. There were a few people that were unhappy with the state of society. They yearned for somebody who would guide the society to the right path. As in the past, was Allah the Almighty going to send a prophet?

Many people were concerned with this issue. The same had occurred in the past ages and on each occasion, Allah had sent a prophet to guide humanity. The prophets proclaimed the right path. Some people believed in them and others denied their messages.

For example Nuh, Salih and Hud were prophets of Allah. Each was sent to a society similar to the people of Mecca, who had strayed from the right path. Allah sent these prophets to warn people and each of them strived to proclaim His law.

Ibrahim was a prophet who strived relentlessly, too. Those who denied his prophethood tried to burn him. However, Allah the Almighty saved him from the fire.

Allah gave books to some prophets. These holy scriptures enlightened people. Allah gave the Torah to the Prophet Musa, the Psalms to the Prophet Dawud and the Bible to the Prophet Isa(Jesus). Each of the prophets invited people to the truth and righteousness.

It had been nearly 600 years since the death of the Prophet Isa. People began to act unjustly and rebel against Allah. The wise men thought that the arrival of a new prophet was near. Everyone was waiting for the new prophet.

# $\mathcal{A}$ Holy Birth

It was the last days in the month of April. Abdulmuttalib was awaiting a grandson. His birth was very soon.

He reflected on recent events and turned to the Ka'bah. What had happened appeared in front of him once more: his confrontation with the gover-

*It was in April, 571. On the 20th day our Prophet was born.*

*Have you not considered how your Lord dealt with the possessors of the elephant? Did He not cause their war to end in confusion, And send down (to prey) upon them birds in flocks, Casting against them stones of baked clay, So He rendered them like straw eaten up?*
*(Surah al-Fil)*

*Did He not find you an orphan and give you shelter?*
*(Duha, 6)*

nor of Yemen, Abraha, who had come to destroy the Ka'bah and the sight of his camels being taken away. While Abraha expected Abdulmuttalib to plead for the Ka'bah he said, "I'm the owner of my camels, and Allah is the owner of the Ka'bah. He will protect it." Allah did protect the Ka'bah and Abdulmuttalib once again felt His greatness.

As he thought of his son Abdullah (Muhammad's father), sorrow had overwhelmed him. It was difficult for him. His son passed away shortly after his marriage to Amina. Now he was waiting the birth of his grandchild.

At that moment someone came running. "Good news Abdulmuttalib! You've just had a grandson." The old man felt his heartbeating rapidly. His eyes were filled with tears of joy.

He ran home. As he entered the house, he heard the sound of a crying infant. He took him in his arms and he felt a mixed feeling of happiness and sorrow. When he kissed him, he remembered his son Abdullah. He wanted to cry, but did not want to cry in front of others. He preferred to cry silently. Abdulmuttalib turned to Amina and asked her what they should name the child. She said, "Muhammad". He became silent. The name was not familiar in their household. Amina explained the dream she saw whereby she was told, "You will give birth to a son. Name him Muhammad." Abdulmuttalib thus named his orphaned grandson Muhammad.

He then took his tiny grandchild to the Ka'bah. He prayed, thanking Allah the Almighty for giving him a grandson. When asked why he named him Muhammad , "So that people and Allah would praise him", he replied.

When Abdulmuttalib returned from the Ka'bah, he saw that his wife and his son Abbas had come to Amina's house. It was a custom to visit the house of the newly born baby. Abbas was only three years old. With a look of astonishment, Abbas gazed at him and touched his face with his small hands. He wanted to kiss him. He then leaned over his cot and kissed Muhammad.

# First Departure

The hot climate of Mecca was not appropriate for raising babies. Thus, many people in Mecca would send their infants to the villages where they were nurtured by a foster mother. This was a source of income in these villages.

*During the Prophet's marriage to Khadijah, Halima came to Mecca to visit him. Our Prophet hugged her and said, "My beloved mother." He asked if she had any needs. Halima told him that there was a severe drought in her region and it had caused much hardship for the inhabitants of the village. He sent her off with a gift of 40 sheep and a camel.*

It had been one week since the birth of Muhammad (saw). In accordance with this custom, Amina was looking for a foster mother. However, most people did not want to take a child whose father had passed away as they thought they would not be able to earn much.

His grandfather was searching as well. He took his grandson in his arms and roamed the streets in search of someone who would accept the infant. It was difficult, yet Abdulmuttalib did not relent. After a long search, he found a lady named Halima and asked, "Would you like to look after an orphan?" Halima did not have any other children to nurse and after discussing with her husband, she accepted the proposal.

Halima took Muhammad (saw) and after preparations, they embarked on a journey. It was a long journey and they finally arrived at her village.

Muhammad (saw) was growing fast and his new sister Shayma and brother Abdullah became accustomed to him. Muhammad (saw) enjoyed the village environment and playing in the fields. He was happy there.

Not before long Halima's husband realised that Muhammad (saw) was a different child. This was because his arrival brought their house more happiness and blessings.

Time was passing rapidly and Muhammad (saw) reached the age of 5. It was time for him to return to his mother Amina. However, Halima and her family had become so accustomed to him that this would be a difficult separation. She took him back to Mecca and when handing him to Amina, she wept. She felt like she was losing her own child. Halima left Mecca to her village in sorrow.

Muhammad (saw) spent his days in Mecca getting accustomed to his mother's household.

Amina's brothers were living in Madinah. So Amina took Muhammad to visit her brothers. His nanny Ummu Ayman came with them as well. They stayed in Madinah for a month and then departed for Mecca. On their arrival at the village of Abwa, Amina became ill.

# His Mother's Last Kiss

In Mecca, Ummu Ayman went searching for Abdulmuttalib. They were able to reach the town after 5 days. How was she going to tell him of her death? At that moment, the sight of Muhammad (saw) appeared in front of her eyes. The orphan now lost his mother as well.

*Our beloved Prophet visited his mother's grave after the Hijrah and fixed it with his own hands. He was unable to hold back his tears and when asked why he was crying he replied, "I cry out my longing for her."*

On finding Abdulmuttalib, she was unable to hide her tears. Abdulmuttalib knew of his daughter-in-law Amina's illness. However, he was anxious because he was unable to receive any further news. He became even more nervous when he did not see Amina with Ummu Ayman. The news was not good. He knew this from the look on her face. Ummu Ayman put her head down and said, "Amina passed away." Abdulmuttalib hugged Muhammad (saw) tightly to relieve his pain.

Ummu Ayman later told him what had happened. They had left Madinah and reached Abwa after a two days' walk. Amina became ill and once she realised that she was living her final moments, she had a talk with her son. She kissed him and then passed away.

After losing his father at Madinah and his mother at Abwa, Muhammad (saw) needed a place of refuge.

It was his grandfather who was to look after him from now on.

# His Grandfather Abdulmuttalib

He lived with his grandfather for two years. They went everywhere together. During the year of severe drought, he even took him to the prayers for rain. He would not sit for dinner without him. Everywhere the two would go, he sit him on the best seat. When asked for the reason he would reply, "In the future, he will become an influential man."

A voice said, "Abdulmuttalib has died." Everyone in the house started crying. Those looking for Muhammad (saw) could see him crying in a corner by himself. The news affected Muhammad (saw) more than anyone else. Abdulmuttalib was like a father to him. His grandfather had treated him with such compassion that he did not feel he had no mother or father.

Muhammad (saw) was crying profoundly. He only came to himself when someone tapped him on his shoulder. When he looked up, he saw it was his uncle Abu Talib. His uncle took him by the hand and raised him to his feet. He rubbed his head and said, "Your grandfather entrusted you to me." From that time on, his uncle was to look after him.

# His Uncle Abu Talib

Muhammad (saw) knew that preparations were being made for a journey to Damascus. The journey could take months. Muhammad (saw) did not want to stay in Mecca without his uncle and asked him to take him as well. Abu Talib said the journey would be long and exhausting. He could become sick and he told him he will not be taking him.

Muhammad (saw) cried and grabbed the saddle of his camel saying, "Uncle, if you go who will I stay here with?"

Abu Talib was touched by his nephew's words and replied, "OK. I will take you with me. From now on the two of us will be inseparable."

From that day on, Abu Talib took his nephew Muhammad (saw) everywhere he went.

Abu Talib had a large family and his financial situation was not good. He and his wife did not want Muhammad (saw) to feel that he was a burden on them. In return, Muhammad (saw) would help his uncle and wife with their affairs. At times he would do their chores, at other times he would look after their livestock and be their shepherd. His aunt would not

*In the later years when his uncle's wife Fatima, the daughter of Esed, died, the Prophet grieved. He said, "Today my mother died." and made her a shroud from his own shirt. When asked about her he would say, "Nobody did more good for me than my uncle Abu Talib and his wife. She was like a mother to me. She would feed me before her own children and comb my hair before she would comb theirs."*

treat him any different than her own children.

Thus, Muhammad (saw) lived in his uncle's household until adulthood.

*When our Prophet was asked whether he worshipped to idols or took alcohol when he was young, he answered "No."*

*He was never mixed up with the wickedness of his society throughout his life.*

# PART 2
# THE YOUNG MUHAMMAD (SAW)

## Unity in Fighting with Injustice

In Mecca, the weak and poor were continually oppressed by the strong and the wealthy. There was a need to change this situation. Thus, the youth of Mecca gathered to discuss this issue.

Muhammad (saw) was amongst those who gathered at the home of Judan, the son of Abdullah. Each was aware of the moral decay of the society. They formed "The Virtue Society". Each member pledged to protect the rights of the people of Mecca and the rights of people who were not from Mecca. They knew that the task ahead of them was a difficult one. Yet, they were determined to strive against injustice.

### Abu Jahl

*His real name was Hisham, the son of Amr. He was one of the leaders of the Quraysh. The Prophet named him Abu Jahl due to his staunch opposition to Islam. Abu Jahl means: the father of ignorance.*

At that moment, a trader from the people of Zabid came to Mecca with three camel loads of goods. Abu Jahl was one of the leaders of Mecca. He intented to buy those goods at an unfairly low price. He proposed a very low deal to the trader. The trader refused to accept the price he offered and Abu Jahl used his influence in Mecca to stop the sales in the local market. The Meccans feared Abu Jahl and he knew he could enforce his will on the people of the town.

The trader was shocked. Someone who saw him in a state of helplessness told him, "Go and see Muhammad (saw), he will get you the price you need." He took heed and went to explain to Muhammad (saw) his predicament. On hearing this, Muhammad (saw) went to the market and purchased all the goods at their fair value. He then went to Abu Jahl's house and strongly warned him not to engage in such action once again. Abu Jahl was surprised by Muhammad's (saw) courage as were the people of Mecca when they heard what had happened.

\*\*\*

In a period where the strong were abusing the weak, someone from Yemen came with his daughter to visit the Ka'bah in Mecca. On entering the town, a man approached to them. He had his eyes set on the girl and his intentions were not good. The father worried and started looking for help. The man kidnapped the girl and he was helpless. Those who heard the father's cry for help told him to go and explain what had happened to the members of the "Virtue Society".

He had no other choice, he went to the Ka'bah shouting, "Is there anybody from the Virtue Society?" All of a sudden, a number of men armed with swords approached him and he became afraid. "What is the matter stranger?" they asked. On hearing the father's plea, the armed men understood that the kidnapper was Nubayh and they headed for his house. On arriving there, they violently knocked the door shouting, "Shame on you Nubayh! Who do you think you are! Bring us this man's daughter immediately!" Nubayh resisted, however the men did not withdraw their demand, "We are not leaving since we have promised each other to fight against injustice. Hand over the girl, otherwise you will suffer the consequences." Nubayh realised he had no other choice but to hand over the girl.

## Road to Marriage

Khadijah was one of the leaders of Mecca and a trader by profession. She realised that she could no longer work on her own. She was in need of someone who was reliable and who could manage some of her work. In a time where there was little trust between people, it became difficult for a woman to work on her own.

The first person that came to her mind was Muhammad (saw). She had heard from his acquaintances that he was a reliable and honest man. And she thought he would be suitable for a career as a trader. Khadijah then sent someone to him to find out his thoughts.

Muhammad (saw) thought about the offer and accepted. Khadijah was to delegate the management of her affairs to Muhammad (saw).

*\*\**

Preparations for the caravan that was headed to Damascus were complete. To help and teach Muhammad (saw) on his first trip, Khadijah sent Maysara with him.

The caravan reached Damascus after an epic journey. Muhammad (saw) made a large profit from the sales of the goods. Also, he bought some goods to sell in Mecca. Maysara got to know Muhammad (saw) better during the trip and was impressed by his integrity and manner.

Maysara gave the entire details of the journey to Khadijah.

# An Exemplary Husband and Father

Khadijah had no doubts about Muhammad's (saw) integrity. He returned with his first caravan in full tact and made a good profit. Everyone would praise his noble character and manner. No one doubted his honesty.

Khadijah had two prior marriages and had many proposals as a widowed lady. She refused each and every one of them. Most of her time was spent on her household and work. This continued till she got to know Muhammad (saw).

Muhammad's (saw) character and personality was attractive and she thought of marrying him. She made a proposal. Muhammad (saw) reached the age of 25 and after considering the proposal for marriage, he accepted it.

The couple had a modest ceremony. After their marriage, Muhammad (saw) moved from his uncle Abu Talib's house to live with Khadijah. He was now a busy trader and his financial situation improved.

Abu Talib was having financial difficulties. In order to support and help raise his son Ali, he accepted him into his home.

Muhammad (saw) and Khadijah loved each other dearly. They had a happy household and were a good example to others. Their first child had brought them joy. Khadijah was now a mother and Muhammad (saw) a father. They named the boy Qasim. Unfortunately, the first child that they loved so dearly passed away in his infancy. After Qasim,

*During the Period of Ignorance when female children were despised, our Prophet would stand up when Fatima arrived, he would kiss her on her cheeks and let her sit in his seat.*

*Abu Lahab and his wife were the staunchest opponents of Islam. Surah al-Lahab was revealed due to the evil they committed against the Muslims. This occurred while the Prophet's two daughters Umm Kulthum and Ruqayya were engaged to Abu Lahab's two sons. On the revelation of this surah, Abu Lahab and his wife forced their sons to divorce their wives. This hurt both the Prophet and Khadijah yet, they remained supportive of their daughters.*

*One of the companions Rafi explains, "When I was a child, I was naughty and would throw stones to date trees. One day the owner of a garden caught me and took me to the Prophet asking him to punish me. The Prophet said, "Why did you stone the date tree my son?"*

*I replied, "I did it because I was hungry."*

*The Prophet said, "Don't stone the date trees my son. Eat from the fruit that has fallen on the ground. Allah will feed you." He rubbed my head and prayed for me, "O Allah, fill his stomach."*

Khadijah gave birth to Zaynab, Umm Kulthum, Ruqayya, Fatima and Abdullah.

\*\*\*

In following years, our beloved Prophet remarried in Madinah after the death of Khadijah. He had a son named Ibrahim from his wife Mariya. When Ibrahim was born, it was a custom to send the new child to a foster mother. Although his son was located at a distant location, our Prophet would regularly visit his son. He would love him and play with him each time.

When Ibrahim was 18 months old, his foster mother informed that he was ill. Muhammad (saw) rushed to her village with a few friends.

Ibrahim was very ill, our Prophet took him in his arms. Ibrahim was living his last moments. He could not bare the sight of his dying child and began to cry. He wept as he kissed his son. The companions were touched by this and were surprised to see him cry. "Why are you crying?" they asked. He replied, "Eyes cry and the heart mourns. I cry out of love for my child. There is no mercy for those who do not have mercy."

The death of a child is the greatest sorrow for a mother or father. The Prophet loved his children dearly and was a man who experienced this sorrow. The Prophet who was raised as an orphan himself was at the funeral of every one of his children except for Fatima.

***

His father had been looking for his son Zayd for years. He knew he had become a slave. However, he had lost all traces of him.

On learning that his son was with Muhammad (saw), he became very worried. He went to Muhammad (saw) crying. The father feared that the Prophet would demand a high price for his son's freedom and was prepared to pay a high price. Muhammad (saw) did not say a word and turned to Zayd:

"You can either stay with me or go with your father." His father was excited. Obviously, he would accept his wishes. Zayd looked at both of them and said:

"Father, I don't want to come. This family did not make me miss you. I found love and peace here. I don't want to leave."

The father was bewildered by his son's assertiveness. How could it be that a slave does not wish to leave his master? Could this be possible? How could a slave be so loyal to his master? He returned to his village empty handed but, with peace inside.

Zayd's loyalty touched Muhammad (saw) and he took him into his household as a foster child.

*His grandchildren were very lucky to have a grandfather like the Prophet. He would joke and play with them and would act like a father.*

*Our Prophet loved his grandson Umama. While he was praying, Umama would climb on his back. He would not get angry and would continue his prayers.*

*The beloved Prophet was so warm to his grandchildren that they would love spending time with him. He would take Hasan and Husain on his back and say, "Kids, your camel is very nice, you two are nice as well."*

*The Prophet was told of the illness of one of his grandchildren. He then went to Zaynab's house. The child was living his last moments. Within moments, the child took his final breaths in his arms. He wept and said, "These tears are the compassion Allah has put in the hearts of people. Allah loves those who are compassionate."*

# Everybody Trusted Him

Muhammad (saw) turned 35. One day, he left home and began walking towards the Ka'bah. Theft, fraud, family feuds were on the rise and there was no sense of trust between people. This saddened him and he wanted to do something to change this situation.

With this thought in mind, he turned to the Ka'bah. The Ka'bah was under repair and he wanted to see how much progress had been made. As he approached the Ka'bah, a group turned to him saying, "There is Muhammad (saw), he is an upright and fair man!" Muhammad (saw) was surprised. He could not understand what had happened. One of the men then turned to him saying:

-As you know, we have been repairing the Ka'bah for a long time. We removed the Black Stone that was named by our forefathers. Now we wish to put it back in its place. But, all the tribes claim the right to this honour. Just as a violent brawl was about to erupt, someone suggested that the first person to walk through the door of Bani Shayba should be allowed to judge on the matter. Everyone accepted this proposal and we were pleased to see you coming through the door. You are the most worthy person in Mecca of this honour. Since we would leave our good in your custody during times when we could not even trust our brothers.

Knowing the significance of the Black Stone, Muhammad (saw) placed it on a large blanket. The tribe leaders held the blanket from each of its corners. When they raised the stone, he picked it up and put it in its place.

The feuding tribes were happy with the outcome and they all praised his ingenuity.

# PART 3
# MUHAMMAD THE MESSENGER

# The First Meeting with Jibreel

When he was in Mecca, Muhammad (saw) would go to the cave of Hira at the mountain of Nour to think and pray. This was his place of shelter. The mountain of Nour was so high that the whole Mecca, including the Ka'bah, could be seen from its summit. He would withdraw to the quietness of the mountain and remain there for days.

On one day he went to Hira and spent the whole night praying. He was tired and the dawn was approaching. As the darkness of the night began to recede, suddenly something appeared. He had never seen such a thing before. It said, "Read." The Prophet Muhammad (saw) got very scared. His hands began to shake and in a fearful force he replied, "I cannot read." It then embraced him violently and left. He

## Peace be on the Prophet

*Allah the Almighty orders Muslims to praise the prophets. Thus, the words "Sallallahu alayhi wa sallam" (peace be upon him) are said on mentioning our Prophet's name. This is an expression of love and respect. It is written in the abbreviated form (saw).*

❧❧❧❀❀❀❦❦❦

thought he would suffocate. Once again the unknown being told him "Read." He replied "I cannot read." On the third occasion, Muhammad (saw) repeated these words that he had been taught:

Read!

In the name of your Lord!

Created man, out of a (mere) clot of congealed blood

Read, for your Lord most bountiful.

He taught man that which he did not know.

*Allah and his angels send blessing on the Prophet: O you that believe! Send your blessings on him, and salute him with all respect.*

*(Ahzab, 56)*

⟫⟫⟫≈❁≈⟪⟪⟪

*The first revelation was received on the Night of Qadr in the year 610.*

⟫⟫⟫≈❁≈⟪⟪⟪

*The first verses revealed were the first 5 verses of Surah al-Alaq.*

⟫⟫⟫≈❁≈⟪⟪⟪

*Alaq refers to the embryo during the creation of the human beings.*

⟫⟫⟫≈❁≈⟪⟪⟪

He was scared and could not understand what had just happened . He came out of the cave. He had to go back to his wife Khadijah. While descending from the mountain, he heard a strong voice, "You are the messenger of Allah and I'm Jibreel." It was the same voice he heard in the cave but it was louder and stronger. A huge being suddenly appeared. It repeated, "You are the messenger of Allah and I'm Jibreel." Muhammad (saw) could not move and his breathing became shallow. He looked up once again to see it repeating the same sentence. He wanted to look away yet, wherever he looked he engulfed by the sight of the angel.

The angel disappeared. Muhammad (saw) was scared. He raced back to Mecca with nervous strides.

# $\mathcal{A}$ Trustworthy Friend Khadijah

With his trembling voice, Muhammad (saw) asked Khadijah to cover his body. Khadijah was unaware of what had occurred. He then fell into a deep sleep.

On waking he, explained to his wife what had happened. Unable to understand the meaning he said, "I was nervous and afraid." Khadijah tried to calm him and replied:

–Do not fear. I swear by Allah that He will never humiliate you. For you honour your kin, you always tell the truth and help the weak. You feed the poor, you are hospitable to your visitors and generous to those in need.

\*\*\*

Khadijah tried to understand what had just happened to her spouse. She knew him well and loved him. Throughout their marriage, she never heard any lies from Muhammad (saw). She believed in him and knew that this was an extraordinary event.

Khadijah's cousin Waraqa was an experienced and wise man. They both went to see him. If there was somebody who would know what had happened, it would be Waraqa.

Waraqa carefully listened to the story and after a profound silence, he replied:

## The Qur'an

*The Qur'an was revealed to Muhammad (saw) in verses and chapters throughout a period of 23 years. It consists of 114 chapters and 6236 verses. The Qur'an is the words of Allah, reading it is worshipping. It contains principles, orders, restrictions and advices for humans to convey happiness to the world life and the afterlife. "Surely this Qur'an guides to that which is most upright and gives good news to the believers who do good that they shall have a magnificent reward."*

*(Isra, 9)*

"The being you saw was the same angel that Allah sent to the Prophet Musa. If only I was younger,I would be with you when the people drives you out of your hometown."

Khadijah and Prophet Muhammad (saw) looked each other in the eye. There was a look on his face that had never been seen before. In a sad tone he asked:

–Are they going to drive me out of Mecca?

Waraqa:

–Yes. Because the prophets that got the same message as yours were all exiled. If I live till that day, I will definitely support you.

Muhammad (saw) was relieved after listening to Waraqa. His wife believed and trusted him. He always relied on her support. Waraqa related some important information and Prophet Muhammad (saw) tried to understand what he had said. He told him that he was facing a new mission. Allah had given him the duty of prophethood. He was 40 years old and he was to invite people to the truth and strive against injustice.

\*\*\*

When the Prophet Muhammad (saw) read the first few verses of the Holy Qur'an and asked "Who will belive me now?", Khadijah lightened his load (even if slightly) by saying, "Even if no-one else belives, I will." Because the Holy Prophet (saw) had been given the heaviest possible responsibilty that could ever be placed upon a human being. The Holy

Prophet Muhammad (saw) was able to overcome the difficulties of the first few days of the revelation owing to the support of his trusting, loyal and understanding wife, Khadijah.

The first people to embrace the new religion were Khadijah and his uncle's son, Ali. Our Prophet began to secretly worship Allah the Almighty together with his family. Simultaneously, they secretly invited the people of Mecca to embrace Islam. On inviting people to Islam, they faced many difficulties and abuse. Regardless of all these, the number of believers grew.

# The Spreading Message

Allah the Almighty wanted our Prophet to warn his family. Thus, he gathered his entire relatives for a meal and after finishing, he invited them to Islam.

Our Prophet's uncle Abu Lahab was defiant and reacted vehemently, "I have never seen anyone inviting his family to such a bad path." On hearing this, they dispersed. The Prophet was determined and made another invitation the following day. At this gathering he talked of the oneness of Allah and that he was his final prophet. His objective was to fulfil the duty that Allah the Almighty had given him.

Our beloved Prophet wanted to proclaim his message to all the people of Mecca. He entered the city square and stood on a high place calling "People of Quraysh!" They began to gather around him. The Prophet (saw) continued:

*And warn your nearest relations,*

*And be kind to them who follows you of the believers.*

*But if they disobey you, then say: Surely I am free of the responsibility what you do.*

*(Shuara, 214-216)*

–If I was to tell you there is an enemy army on the other side of this hill, would you all believe me?

In unison they replied:

–Yes. We have never heard you lie before.

He continued:

–I swear by Allah that one day you will all die and be resurrected to give an account for all of what you have done. There is paradise for the good and hell for the bad. I have been given the duty to warn you of the difficulty on the Day of Judgement. Those who believe in the oneness of Allah and my prophethood will be saved on that day. Those who do not believe will be subjected to much hardship. Are you ready to support me in this call?

Those who gathered were bemused. Abu Lahab displayed his enmity once more and hurled a stone at our beloved Prophet shouting:

–Did you gather us here to talk such nonsense?

Although he may not have succeeded in finding new adherents, the people of Mecca were made aware of the great call of Islam.

# The House of Arqam

Umar, the son of Hattab, was a strong and courageous man. Nobody would dare confront him and most people who saw him would walk the other way. He heard that Muhammad (saw) had announced his prophethood and decided to murder him. On his way to the Prophet, he met Nuaym. Nuaym became a Muslim, however, he did not reveal this to anyone. When he saw Umar in such an angry state:

–Where are you going, he enquired. Umar replied:

–I'm going to kill Muhammad.

Nuaym became cautious:

–Well, you have a hard task ahead of you.

In order to protect the Prophet (saw) and divert Umar's attention he added:

–I would be more worried about your sister and brother in law if I were you. They have also become Muslims. Umar became furious and left to his sister's house.

On arriving, he heard a recitation. He realised that they had both become Muslims. He raided their house.

Without giving them a chance to realise what had happened, he grabbed and threw both of them in either direction of the room. He was in such a rage that he drew his sword at his sister who cried aloud:

–Fear Allah Umar. Let it be known to you as well that we became Muslims. Regardless of what you do, we will not revoke our religion.

Umar was surprised with her brave defiance in the face of his sword. How dare she oppose the sword of Umar. He could not understand why he momentarily paused. He began to feel the hand holding his sword tremble. He sat down. Then he asked what his sister was reciting. Once she noticed Umar was calmer, she brought a copy of the verses they were reciting.

## The Abyssinian Bilal

*Bilal was a slave who became a Muslim. His master subjected him to torture because he had embraced Islam without his consent. He took Bilal out to the hot sands of the desert and placed a giant stone on his chest threatening, "If you don't give up your religion, I will kill you in this manner." In the face of this grave torture, he still proclaimed, "Allah is one and the greatest!"*

## Torture to the Prophet

*Of the Companions Munbit explains, "I saw Allah's messenger and he said "If you say 'la ilaha illallah', you will be saved. " When people heard this, some spat on him, others threw dirt on him and some shouted abuse. This continued till the afternoon. At that moment, his daughter Zaynab arrived with a cup of water. She was crying. He washed his hands and face and had some to drink. Turning to her he said, "Don't cry my dear. Definitely, Allah will protect your father."*

His sister and brother in law were surprised at Umar's change. He began to read the verses. He continued to read and it was obvious that he was affected. He became a new Umar. He asked about the house of Arqam and then left.

During the time when the believers in Allah were limited in number, Prophet Muhammad (saw) searched for a place to gather. Arqam's house was on the outskirts of Mecca and did not attract the attention of foreigners. He would gather there with his friends.

Nuaym came running to Arqam's house. He explained that Umar was keen on killing the Prophet. All those in the house were ready to protect the Prophet at all cost, even if their own lives.

On Umar's arrival, there was a profound silence at Arqam's house. He entered and said that he came to see the Prophet. The Prophet asked him to approach. Umar came slowly, knelt on the floor and uttered the following words:

–There is no god but Allah, Muhammad is the messenger of Allah.

Those present at Arqam's house were shocked. Umar became become a Muslim.

The conversion of Umar strengthened the Muslims. They went in a group to the Ka'bah to perform prayers. There was no longer a need to hide their beliefs. Their numbers were growing rapidly. They could no longer fit in Arqam's house.

The Islamic call had to be conveyed outside of Mecca as well. The Prophet began to visit communities outside the town. There were times when he was seen favourable and times when he was subjected to the harshest of abuse. Nevertheless, our Prophet continually strived to proclaim the message of Islam without becoming despondent or helpless.

# The Suppression Begins

The number of people embracing the Islamic call was growing rapidly. This made the pagans anxious. They wanted to destroy the morale of the Muslims and prevent the growth of Islam by systematically ridiculing the believers. They began to publicly hassle and verbally abuse Muslims. When they saw the beloved Prophet, they would say, "Look, there is the man who gets messages from the sky." They did not stop there. Although they knew the Prophet very well, they called him insane, a magician and a fortune teller. Their opposition was so strong that they went as far as attempting murder.

Yet, they were still unable to prevent the growing number of the believers. Muslims would not give up their beliefs. The pagans were helpless. The leaders of Mecca organised a meeting with the Prophet's uncle Abu Talib, and talked about him on recent developments and asked him to convince his nephew. They told him:

–Tell your nephew to abandon this cause.

### The first martyrs

*Yasir and his wife Sumayyah became Muslims. When people heard that they became Muslims, they were subjected to torture. They had no helpers because they were poor and weak. They were devoted to their convictions. Abu Jahl subjected them to enormous hardship as they continued to practice their religion without compromise. He eventually martyred them with arrows once he realised he could not convince them to abandon their beliefs.*

*Yasir and Sumayyah were the first Muslims to be martyred for their beliefs.*

Abu Talib called his nephew and conveyed their demands. The Prophet's reply was:

–If you were to put the sun in my right hand and the moon in my left, I still will not abandon this cause till the day I die.

Abu Talib knew about the injustices of the Meccans and was impressed by the Prophet's determination. He did not want him to be harmed and continued to support him :

–Rest assured. They will not harm you as long as I live.

\*\*\*

Once they realised that they could not convince the Prophet to abandon the cause, the pagans of Mecca resorted to a new ploy. They signed a pact amongst themselves and posted it on the walls of Ka'bah.

According to the agreement; all the people were to disassociate with the Prophet's family and all Muslims until they hand him over dead or alive. The Prophet's family and the Muslims were announced as enemies. No one was to marry them, engage in business or even talk to them.

This was the beginning of a long and difficult period for the Muslims. They could not trade, buy or sell anything. Yet, they still refused to hand over the Prophet to the Meccan elite and continue to protect him at all cost even if their own lives.

The boycott lasted three years and the Meccan pagans eventually capitulated. A number of people, including some of the Prophet's relatives, removed the sign on the Ka'bah wall to signify the end of the boycott. The boycott had only strengthened the Muslims.

## The year of sorrow

Muslims were relieved once the boycott ended. Within a couple of months, there were two important events that saddened our beloved Prophet; the death of his uncle Abu Talib and his wife Khadijah. Both were loyal followers and had provided him with great support in times of hardship. "I do not know which of these hardships on my Ummah will hurt me the most.", he reflected. It was a year of sorrow for him.

# Search for a New Homeland

## Abyssinia

Life became very difficult in Mecca. As the oppression on Muslims intensified, the Prophet turned in search for a new homeland. Initially he allowed a group of fifteen people to emigrate to Abyssinia. This was the first emigration. The pagans then made it more difficult for the remaining Muslims to practice Islam. This was followed a year later by an arrival of another 100 Muslims at Abyssinia. In order to prevent this trend, the pagans of Mecca sent a group of envoys to the Abyssinian king.

The representatives of the Meccan elite arrived in the Abyssinian Najashi's court with expensive gifts and presents. When asked who they were, they replied:

### Khadijah

*The love of our Prophet for Khadijah was so great that he never forgot her even after her death. He would always remember her for her friendship, support and sacrifice, as she was a believer at a time when most people denied his prophethood. The Prophet's latter wife Aisha knew this and envied her.*

–We are from Mecca. We came to seek the return of fugitives who have sought refuge in your land.

In response he asked:

–Why is it that you seek these people?

"These people have rejected the religion of our forefathers and they claim to believe another religion which they preach in our land." they replied.

After a brief moment of silence, Najashi rose to his feet. He considered returning these refugees to the pagans. However, such an act would violate his principles of justice and fairness. He had to listen to the accused. The monarch summonsed the Muslims to his court.

Najashi conveyed these claims to the Muslims and asked if they had anything they would like to say in response. On hearing this Jafar, the son of Abu Talib, stepped forward to say:

–We were evil. Allah sent a righteous and a trustworthy prophet from among us. This prophet invited us to teach and worship only Allah and abandon the worship of idols. He ordered us to be truthful, to honour our neighbors and kin, and to end all blood feuds. He banned us from immorality, lying and baring false witness, taking away the goods of orphans and making false accusations against honourable women. He ordered us only to worship Allah and not to worship anyone else. And we believed and accepted his message. Whatever Allah

ordered him, we followed. We accepted the lawful as lawful. However, we were oppressed and tortured in order to change our religion. Thus, we had no other alternative than to seek refuge in your land.

Najashi listened carefully. He asked Jafar about the verses revealed by Allah. Once Jafar recited some verses from the Surah Maryam, he realised what the Meccan envoys said was not true. He said that he will not hand over the Muslims to the Meccans and that they are free to settle anywhere in his land. Najashi sent the group together with their gifts back to Mecca.

## Taif

A month after the death of Khadijah, the Prophet went to the town of Taif with his foster son Zayd. His aim was to preach Islam to new people.

The Prophet told the Taif crowd of the existence and oneness of Allah, and that he was the final prophet. The people of Taif reacted angrily and spoke abusively against the Prophet. The slaves and youth of the town threw stones at our Prophet and Zayd. Zayd desperately tried to protect the Prophet from the countless stones to no avail. His body was wounded and began to bleed. The two could not stand on their feet any longer and had to rest under the shade of a distant tree. Our Prophet said:

–Oh Allah! I am weak and helpless. I only turn to you from my helplessness to people. Oh Allah! You are the protector of the weak. You are truly strong and will protect your believers from evil.

Our Prophet did not even condemn those that subjected him to hardship because, he was the Prophet of compassion and mercy.

## Aqaba: The road leading to Madinah

While the beloved Prophet ignored the hardships imposed on him, he continued to preach the message of Islam and he was in search of a homeland where Muslims could live in peace and harmony.

The Prophet met a group of people who arrived from the town of Madinah. He preached the message and the six of them became Muslims. The group agreed to meet the Prophet during the upcoming Hajj season. When they returned to Mecca with another six people, 12 in total, they pledged "not to worship anyone other than Allah, not to steal, not to commit adultery, not to take the lives of their infant daughters and not to falsely accuse anyone". The group secretly agreed to meet a year later and the Prophet sent his friend Musab bin Umeyr to Madinah with them to preach Islam.

The following year, the Muslims of Madinah returned to Mecca with a group of 75 people. They met with the Prophet at Aqaba secretly. The Prophet came to Aqaba with his uncle, Abbas. Abbas turned to the new Muslims of Madinah and said:

### The miracle of Isra and Miraj

*After a three-year boycott and the loss of his wife and uncle followed by the return from Taif empty handed, the sorrow of the Prophet peaked. He prayed to Almighty Allah to help him in these days of hardship.*

*When praying at the Ka'bah one night, the angel Jibreel took the Prophet from Mecca to the Aqsa Mosque in Jerusalem. They then ascended to the heavens together. This is known as the miracle of Isra and Miraj. This event happened in a short time and the Prophet returned to Mecca before dawn.*

*Allah the Almighty ordered the Prophet and Muslims the 5 daily prayers at the Miraj.*

꒰꒱꒰꒱꒰꒱

–He is my brother's son and I love him dearly. We are protecting him here in Mecca but, I fear his safety in Madinah. If you are confident that you can protect him there, then let him come with you. If not, let him stay in Mecca.

Our Prophet added to the words of his uncle Abbas:

–What I ask from you is only to worship Allah. For myself; I ask you to protect me and my friends.

He then recited verses from the Qur'an.

The people of Madinah promised to protect the Prophet and his friends as they protected their kin, to be on the side of good and advise against evil. Once they invited the Prophet to Madinah, the Muslims were ordered to migrate to Madinah.

## Prayer

*The five daily prayers are an obligation on every sane and mature Muslim male and female. It is a great sin to neglect prayer without a valid reason. The Jumuah prayer is also obligatory, and Ramadan and sacrifice prayers are wajib. It is a great sin not to perform daily prayers without an acceptable excuse.*

*«Recite that which has been revealed to you of the Book and keep up prayer; surely prayer keeps (one) away from indecency and evil, and certainly the remembrance of Allah is the greatest, and Allah knows what you do.»*
*(Ankabut, 45)*

# PART 4
# JOURNEY TO MADINAH

## We are Going in order to Return

The disbelievers plotted against the Holy Prophet (saw) as Islam spread beyond Mecca. They planned to camouflage the would-be-killer amongst them by including fighters from each of their tribes. The Holy Prophet (saw), upon news of their evil attack, had plans of his own.

The Beloved Prophet and his dear friend Abu Bakr reached the cave of Thawr nearby Mecca. Ali remained in Mecca to return the goods in the custody on the Prophet to the Meccans. To disguise their departure, Ali slept in the Prophet's bed that night. Abu Bakr's son Abdullah was to inform them of the activities in Mecca. Also, the shepherd Amir drove

*Our Prophet and Abu Bakr were hiding in the Thawr cave while a group of people were in search of them. They came to the entrance of the cave where they were hiding. If the group had bended and looked through, they would have seen and caught them, but Allah protected.*

**The Holy Qur'an describes the Hijrah as follows:**

*If you will not aid him, Allah certainly aided him when those who disbelieved expelled him, he being the second of the two, when they were both in the cave, when he said to his companion: Grieve not, surely Allah is with us. So Allah sent down His tranquility upon him and strengthened him with hosts which you did not see, and made lowest the word of those who disbelieved; and the word of Allah is the highest; and Allah is Mighty, Wise.*

*(Tawbah, 40)*

his flock to the vicinity of the cave to bring them milk as well as to hide the footprints Abdullah had left behind. On the third day Uraykid's son Abdullah would arrive at the cave with two camels to guide them for the journey ahead.

The following day, Abdullah secretly came to Thawr to bring news from Mecca:

–The pagans were surprised to find Ali in the Prophet's bed that night. They abused him and he was imprisoned for a while. Once they realized he had nothing to say, he was released and an announcement was made that a reward of 100 camels would be given to whoever captures the two of you dead or alive. Thus, everybody is searching for you.

The people who could not find him in his house were in search of him everywhere. At last, one group came to the entrance of the cave where they were hiding. If the group had bended and looked through, they would have seen and caught them. Allah protected them with his invisible army. The group left without seeing them. It was the third day in the cave. At the approach of dawn, Uraykid's son Abdullah arrived as planned and they departed for Madinah.

It was very difficult for the Prophet to leave the town where he was born and spent the days of his childhood and youth. He was to leave behind all his memories of pleasure and pain, hopes and dreams. Also, the oppression of the Meccans continued and it was impossible to freely practise the commands of Allah. However, Madinah was a door to hope. The Muslims would be able to freely practise and preach Islam. As he rode his camel to Madinah, the Prophet was contemplating this and halted for a moment looking back to Mecca saying:

–Mecca, you are the most beautiful town on earth. If they had not separated me from you, I would not have abandoned you. One day, I shall return.

Waraqa's words came true. The Prophet was forced to leave his hometown at the age of 53.

# They were Waiting for Him

It had been eight days since our beloved Prophet and his road companion Abu Bakr had left the cave of Thawr. They would rest during the scorching heat of the day and continue on their journey at night. After an epic journey, they arrived at the village of Quba, three kilometres from Madinah.

The Muslims of Madinah received the news of the Prophet's imminent arrival. Every day, they would climb to the high grounds outside of the town and wait for him. They did not receive any news after his departure from Mecca, therefore it was an anxious wait.

*Umar was a courageous man. He could not take it upon himself to leave Mecca in secret. So he armed himself with his sword together with a bow and arrow and went to the Ka'bah. Turning to people:*

*–Pagans! I am emigrating to Madinah. Whosoever wants his children to be orphaned, his wife to be widowed and his mother to be left in tears can come, I will fight him behind that mountain. I will be waiting." No one from the crowded had the courage to respond to his call.*

*During the Hijrah, the Prophet gave a sermon and prayed together with up to 100 Muslims at the valley of Ranuna. This was the first Jumuah prayer. The mosque at that site is known as the Jumuah Mosque today.*

On another day while gazing from the outskirts of Madinah, they saw two people approaching. It was the Prophet and Abu Bakr.

The youngsters and the elders of Madinah were delighted with his arrival. The children started singing, "Welcome beloved Prophet, welcome!" Madinah was in a carnival mode.

When the Prophet entered Madinah, everybody was competing with each other to have him as a guest at their house. However, he let his camel free and said he will stay at the house closest to where the

animal halts to rest. The camel roamed the streets of Madinah until it found a vacant block of land and sat close to Abu Ayyub al-Ansari's house. He was delighted to have both the Prophet and Abu Bakr as guests at his house.

Our beloved prohet stayed at Abu Ayyub's house for a while.

**When the Prophet arrived in Madinah, the girls of the town sang him this song:**

**THE MOON ROSE ABOVE US**
The moon rose above us
From the hills of Wadaa
We must be thankful
Of the call to Allah

You are the sun,
You are the moon
You are light upon light
You are the star of Surayya
Oh beloved, Oh Messenger

Oh the one raised amongst us
You came with a great calling
You honoured this town
Oh beloved, Oh Messenger

Abu Ayyub, who hosted our beloved Prophet, died in Istanbul while he came for the conquest of the city and his tomb is near the Eyyub Sultan Mosque.

PART 5

# MADINAH:
# A CIVILIZATION CITY

## A New Civilization is Born

The ancient name of Madinah was Yathrib. It was a town of considerable importance prior to the beloved Prophet's emigration, too. Arab and Jewish communities lived side by side in the town that hosted various religious groups. There were no unity between the tribes and there were ongoing disputes among them.

## Mosque

The first duty of our beloved Prophet in Madinah was to build a mosque.

A mosque is not merely a place of worship. It is an educational institution, a social centre, a place where the community needs are discussed and the poor and needy are cared for.

*On arrival in Madinah, the Prophet built a mosque in the place where his camel initially laid to rest. Its name is the Prophet's Mosque (al-Masjid al-Nabawi).*

# Adhan

**Adhan**
*Allahu Akbar
(4times)
Ash-hadu an la ilaha
illallah
(2 times)
Ash-hadu anna
Muhammadan
Rasulullah
(2 times)
Hayya alas salah
(2 times)
Hayya alal falah
(2 times)
Allahu Akbar
(2 times)
La ilaha illallah
(once)*

*English:
Allah is the greatest
I bear witness there
is no god but Allah
I bear witness that
Muhammad is the
prophet of Allah
Come to prayer
Come to salvation
Allah is the greatest
There is no god but
Allah*

The number of Muslims was growing, the mosque was at full capacity and unable to house the increasing number of believers. There was a need to announce the times of prayer and to call the believers to worship. The Christians would use a church bell and Jews would use a trumpet, therefore it was inappropriate to use any of these methods. Lighting a fire or raising a flag was not appropriate either.

The issue was resolved when Abdullah, the son of Zayd, and other companions told the Prophet various dreams they had seen. Abdullah told of the call of the adhan that he had dreamt and the Prophet verified that this was taught to him by revelation. The Prophet then directed Bilal to make the call to payer as he had a pleasant and resonate voice.

Bilal was reciting the adhan and was calling the Muslims to prayer with his beautiful voice.

# Settlement

The Prophet devised a settlement plan for the new emmigrants to Madinah. The Muslims of Madinah that had numerous blocks of land donated them and the Prophet facilitated the settlement of the new emmigrants to the town.

# Brotherhood

The Beloved Prophet knew very well that Muslims had to live in harmony. The Muslims that migrated from Mecca were known as the "The Muhajireen" (The Emigrants), and those originally from Madinah were referred to as "The Ansar" (The Helpers). The Emigrants were in a foreign land. They had left all their belongings in Mecca, some had left their families and children behind. The Prophet thus announced the brotherhood of the Emigrants and the Helpers. Each chose a brother for themselves. This relieved much of the burden on the Emigrants and the Helpers were delighted with the privilege to help.

Thus, the Prophet was able to establish unity among the Muslims and a strong community in the face of internal and external strife.

# Living side by side

The pagans of Mecca were looking for an opportunity to attack Madinah. The united Muslim community also felt the need to forge alliances with other groups.

Madinah was a town of 10 000 inhabitants. A large part of them were Jews and they were a great power. Also, there were non-Muslim Arabs living in the town. The Prophet negotiated a peace treaty with these groups and all sides agreed to live in harmony amongst each other.

In accordance with the treaty, Muslims and Jews were to have equal rights and if a Jew was harmed, both

*• A Muslim is a Muslim's brother. He does not harm him and will not hand him over to his enemy. Whosoever relieves the burden of his brother, Allah will relieve his burden. Whosoever saves his brother from hardship, Allah will save him from the hardship of the Day of Judgement. Whosoever does not reveal the faults of his brother, Allah will not reveal his faults on the Day of Judgement.*

*• The best of you is he who is best in character.*

*• Do not stray from truthfulness, as truthfulness is the road to goodness, and goodness is the road to paradise. Turn from falsehood, as falsehood is the road to evil, and evil is the road to the hellfire.*

*•Those who sleep while their neighbour is hungry are not one of us .*

**Hadith**
*These are the words of our Prophet. After the Qur'an, the hadith is the second source of Islamic knowledge.*

**Hadith from the Riyadh as-Saliheen Collection**

*• Islam is based on 5 foundations: believing that there is no god other than Allah, believing that Muhammad is the servant and messenger of Allah, performing prayer, almsgiving , fasting in Ramadan and pilgrimage if one is able.*

*• The best of the people is he, who is the most helpful to others.*

*• Paradise is under the feet of mothers.*

*• Cleanness is a part of iman (faith).*

*• He, who does not have compassion for the young and respect for the elders is not one of us.*

Muslims and Jews would provide support. The same would apply to Muslims. Both sides also agreed to defend the town together in the event of an external attack.

The Prophet would be a mediator in any dispute between the parties, who were free to practice their own religion.

The contract finished the civil war in Madinah. At the end, the advantegeous side was our Prophet and the Muslims.

## All went to school

Near the Mosque of the Prophet, an area where students could sleep was built. This was known as the Suffa. It was a school and the teacher was the Prophet. He instructed them in the Qur'an and other matters. The students were taught as well as given instruction on how to teach.

## Ramadan

The month of Ramadan is the month of worship. It is the order of Allah to spend this month in fasting.

Fasting was ordered one and a half years after the hijrah with the following verse: "O you who believe! Fasting is prescribed for you, as it was prescribed for those before you, so that you may guard (against evil)." (Baqarah, 183)

Our Prophet emphasised the importance of this month. He would fast during the day and worship extensively during the night. He would help the needy, clothe and feed the poor.

The Qur'an was revealed on the Night of Qadr during this month. During this month, Muslims should spend time worshipping, performing tarawih, making prayers, reciting the Qur'an and engaging in charity.

Wealthy Muslims should devote a certain portion of their wealth as almsgiving. Almsgiving is one of the five fundamental obligations of Islam and was

*Fasting was ordered one and a half years after the Hijrah with the following verse: "O you who believe! fasting is prescribed for you, as it was prescribed for those before you, so that you may guard (against evil)." (Baqarah, 183)*

*And there are some among them who say: Our Lord! grant us good in this world and good in the hereafter, and save us from the chastisement of the fire.*
*(Baqarah, 201)*

*O our Lord! Grant me protection and my parents and the believers on the day when the reckoning shall come to pass!*
*(Ibrahim, 41)*

ordered two years after the Hijrah. It is mentioned together with prayer many times: "And keep up prayer and pay the poor-rate and bow down with those who bow down." (Baqarah, 43)

# The Enmity Continues

The period spent in Mecca was a time of patience. The Muslims were continually oppressed by the pagans and forced to endure their oppression. The Beloved Prophet advised the Muslims to persevere and not to react in violence. The pagans however, persisted in making life difficult for them in the town.

The Muslims then were able to establish their state in Madinah and live in peace and harmony with their neighbors. The Prophet spread the message of Islam by peaceful means and did not support the use of force or war. He called people to read the Qur'an and educate themselves. People were to enter the fold of Islam by their free will.

The pagans of Mecca were violently opposed to the spread of Islam and were secretly preparing to wage war on the Muslims. In order to prevent such a threat, the Prophet sought to take control of the Meccan trade route. The trade convoy included a stash of weapons as well and the Prophet knew these would be used against the Muslims of Madinah.

## The turning point: Badr

The probability of going to war with Mecca grew day by day and this disturbed the Prophet.

After making preparations, the Prophet journeyed with over 300 of his companions to the wells of Badr. The pagans prepared an army of 1000 and were on their way .

At this moment, Huzayfa reached the Prophet to inform him that he and his father had been captured by the Meccans on their way to join the Muslim army. The pagans released them once they promised not to join the Muslims.

The Prophet was in need of soldiers. Yet, he ordered them to remain loyal to their promise and return to Madinah and not to participate in the battle.

*Remember When you sought aid from your Lord, so He answered you: I will assist you with a thousand of the angels following one another.*
*(Anfal, 9)*

As the Prophet saw a strong pagan army approaching from the distance, he prayed:

"Oh Allah, that is the Quraysh. They approach in arrogance, rebel against you and deny your prophet.

*At Badr, the Prophet had a thought regarding the hostages of war. He said: "Of those who are literate, they will be set free if they teach ten Muslims to read and write." In this way, not only the prisoners of war would get their freedom but also Muslim children would learn how to read and write.*

⟫⟩⟩⟩⟩⟩❀❀⟨⟨⟨⟨⟨

*After the victory at Badr, the voice of the Muslims was heard throughout the Arabian Peninsula. The era of spreading Islam began.*

⟫⟩⟩⟩⟩⟩❀❀⟨⟨⟨⟨⟨

O Allah, help us! If you allow this small number of Muslims to be annihilated, there will be no people left on earth to worship you."

On reaching Badr, the Prophet ordered his army to take positions. The place they took was sandy. One of Prophet's friends Hubab turned him to ask:

–Is this an order from Allah or is it your decision?

On replying that it was his decision, Hubab added:

–This is not an appropriate position to wage war from. Allow us to take positions next to the wells. Let us close off the other wells nearby as well.

Thus, the decision was made to take positions at the water source and close off the nearby wells.

The Prophet then turned to the Ansar and Muhajireen to enquire on their thoughts regarding the imminent battle. Both groups confirmed their allegiance.

Although preparations were complete, the Prophet was still opposed to engaging in war. He then sent Umar to the pagan army as an envoy in order to dissuade them from entering the battle. The Meccans thought otherwise. Their impression was that the opposing army was weak and that this was a great opportunity to rid the Arabian peninsula of the Muslims' presence. Under no circumstance were they to abandon war.

The battle reached a conclusion in five hours. The pagan army was dealt an ominous blow. The Muslims lost 14 soldiers whereas the Meccans lost 70 men, including the most prominent of them Abu Jahl. Allah the Almighty sent his help and accepted the Prophet's prayer.

# A sorrowful experience: Uhud

Another year passed. New news of an imminent attack by the Meccans reached Madinah. The Muslims gathered to discuss the matter. At the meeting, Hamza voiced his opinion that the battle to be waged outside the town. A number of youths supported Hamza. The Prophet however, was of the view that the town should be defended from within. The matter went to a vote and the Prophet accepted the majority decision of meeting the enemy outside of Madinah.

Soon, the news of a fully equipped army of 3000 men had reached the outskirts of Madinah was received. The Meccans came to take the revenge of Badr.

The Prophet and his companions departed after Friday prayer. The following morning, they arrived at the mountain of Uhud. They numbered 1000 however, 300 of them deserted the army while on the road. This group appeared to be Muslims but, were not believers at heart. Their objective was to scare and demoralize the Muslims and they are known as the Hypocrites.

It was the year 625. The two armies met at the mountain of Uhud near Madinah. The pagans reached very close to Madinah with the objective of ransacking the town once they defeated the Muslims. Our prophet was aware of this and had taken precautions concerning the most minute of matters. He chose fifty of the best marksmen and positioned

*At the battle of Uhud, the commander of the pagan army Abu Sufyan made this proposal to the Ansar:*

*–People of Madinah. We have no issue with you. Allow us to engage face to face with Muhammad.*

*The proposal was fiercely opposed.*

*When the Prophet was wounded at the battle of Uhud, his companions wanted him to pray for Allah to curse the pagans, but our Prophet said:*

*–I was not sent to curse anybody. I was sent as a prophet of mercy to guide people. May Allah show them the right path as they know not the truth.*

them on the left flank of a hilltop. He put them under the command of Abdullah, the son of Jubayr and advised them:

–Protect us from the pagan horsemen. Do not allow them to manoeuvre and attack us from behind. Whether we win or lose the battle, under no circumstances are you to leave your positions. Even if you see us killed, do not come to help us.

The battle began and within a few hours, the pagans were dealt with a heavy blow. However, the tide of the battle changed in a short time. The Muslims were stranded between two groups of pagans as the marksmen had deserted their positions with the thought that the battle was won.

The price of not adhering to the Prophet's advise was heavy. Seventy Muslims lost their lives including Hamza. Our beloved Prophet's lip was wounded and he lost a tooth. The Muslims were able to salvage the battle by seeking the refuge of the Mount Uhud. The Meccans withdrew with the thought that the loss at Badr had been avenged.

When the Muslims descended from the hill, they saw that the bodies of the martyred Muslims were tortured and mutilated. After burying the dead in sorrow, they returned to Madinah.

Because of these archers, who had not taken our Prophet's warnings into consideration, the result of the war was a loss instead of victory. By not obeying the commander, Muslims paid a great price in this war.

# All means are tried: Assassinations

The pain of Uhud was felt in the streets of Madinah. The Muslims were hurt by the battle, but they were still with the Prophet. They fully realised the importance of adhering to his advise and daily life continued as usual.

Meanwhile, a man came to Madinah asking the Prophet for a number of teachers to be sent to his people. The Prophet asked him to promise that his people would protect these teachers. Once the man made the pledge, the Prophet dispatched seventy of his companions who were trained at the Suffa school.

Seventy of them were murdered in an ambush at the location of Biri Maun while they had no chance of protecting themselves.

\*\*\*

Also, an ambush was staged at the site of Raji. Eight Muslims were murdered here and Hubab and Zayd were taken as captives and sold to the Meccans. Hubab was murdered by the Meccans and Zayd was asked as follows before his death:

–Would you prefer that Muhammad was in your position now?

–Forget about him being here now, I cannot stand the sight of a thorn on his foot.

The pagans were amazed at the devotion that they could not stop saying what a great love his companions had for him that they had never seen this kind of love before.

# A though test: Khandak (Trench)

***Khandak digging***

*Jabir narrates:*
*– While digging the trench, we came across a very hard surface. On informing the Prophet, he took the sledge hammer in his hands and struck the trench.  None of us had eaten for 3 days, including the Prophet. He hit the rock so hard that it disintegrated like sand.*

Two years passed since the battle of Uhud. The news was that the Meccans had dispatched an army of ten thousand. The pagans were still uncomfortable with the Muslim presence in Madinah. The Prophet immediately gathered his companions in the mosque to discuss preparations for war.

The Persian Salman said:

–In Persia, we would dig a trench around our town in such a situation. Let us do the same.

The majority agreed. A trench was to be dug around Madinah within one week at the latest. Work began before daybreak every day and continued till sunset. The Prophet joined the effort and provided moral support to his companions.

Within a week, a trench of five kilometers was dug. The width of trench was sufficient enough to prevent a horse from passing and deep enough to not allow a fallen horse from climbing out. The army was put into battle mode and the pagan forces arrived. They had the support of the Jews, as well as the non-Muslim Arabs of Madinah. However, they were totally surprised at the site of the trench as they had never seen one before.

The battle began. It intensified then dissipated at times. After a siege of twenty seven days, the pagans were still unable to achieve an outcome. The battle ended in another victory of the Muslims.

***The Holy Qur'an describes the battle of Khandak as follows:***

*O you who believe! Call to mind the favour of Allah to you when there came down upon you hosts, so We sent against them a strong wind and hosts, that you saw not, and Allah is Seeing what you do.*

*When they came upon you from above you and from below you, and when the eyes turned dull, and the hearts rose up to the throats, and you began to think diverse thoughts of Allah. There the believers were tried and they were shaken with severe shaking. (Ahzab, 9,10,11)*

# PART 6
# RETURNING HOME

## The Treaty of Hudaybiyyah

Our beloved Prophet was very happy that day. He explained his joy to his companions: "Tomorrow, we will visit the Ka'bah and Mecca." It had been six years since leaving the town they missed dearly. They were to walk in the streets of Mecca and relive the days of their childhood and youth.

Our Prophet traveled to Mecca with 1500 companions and visited the grave of his mother on the road.

They reached the site of Hudaybiyyah, near Mecca where they set camp. Our Prophet designated Uthman as an envoy to the Meccans to tell them that they did not come to declare war and that they wanted permission to visit the Ka'bah. On visiting the holy site, they were to return home. Uthman went to meet the Meccans, however his return was delayed. There was news that he was murdered.

*Certainly Allah was well pleased with the believers when they pledged allegiance to you under the tree, and He knew what was in their hearts, so He sent down tranquillity on them and rewarded them with a near victory, And many acquisitions which they will take; and Allah is Mighty, Wise.*

*(Fath, 18,19)*

They did not come for war yet, there was a possibility that war may break out. Our Prophet gathered his companions. They pledged to support the Prophet till death.

Soon, news was received that Uthman was alive. He arrived together with a representative of the Meccan pagans.

The Meccan envoy stated that they would not allow the Muslims to enter Mecca and that they wanted to negotiate a treaty. After the meeting, they accepted the terms of the treaty that was signed by both parts. The Muslims were not happy. They were unable to enter the town after traveling so far.

According to the treaty, the Muslims were not to enter Mecca and pray at the Ka'bah until the following year. What upset the Muslims most was that the treaty included unfavorable conditions. When members of the Quraysh became Muslims and sought refuge in Madinah, they were not to be granted asylum and were to be returned to the pagans. However, when anybody from Madinah seeks refuge in Mecca, he was not to be granted asylum and returned. The Muslims were offended and feared for their lives.

Soon, a person with chains around his neck and feet arrived. He was exhausted and soaked in sweat and blood. It was Abu Jandal. Suhayl imprisoned and chained his son because he had become a Muslim. He was able to escape but, his father grabbed him by his chains and beat him across the face. Turning to the Prophet he said:

–The agreement was signed before my son arrived.

Our Prophet quietly confirmed. Suhayl demanded the return of his son as Abu Jandal cried out:

–Muslims! How can you allow them to torture and force me to abandon the Religion?

Our Prophet took the father of Abu Jandal aside and requested him to free his son. However, he vehemently refused. Thus, the Prophet turned to Abu Jandal:

– Have patience Abu Jandal. Allah will definitely save you and your friends. We signed an agreement with these people. We gave them our word and they gave us theirs. We cannot revoke the agreement, and sent him back to Mecca.

These events deeply hurt the Muslims, however, the pagans officially recognized them with this treaty.

# $\mathcal{A}$im: The Entire World

The setting for peace and harmony was established once the Treaty of Hudaybiyyah was signed. Our Prophet made the best use of this opportunity. He sent letters to Heraclius of the Byzantia, Kisra of Persia and various other leaders. He invited all to embrace Islam.

The objective was to disseminate the Islamic message to the entire world.

*And We have not sent you but as a mercy to the worlds.*

*(Anbiya, 107)*

*** 

An envoy presented the letter to the Byzantine Emperor Heraclius. He opened the letter and began to read:

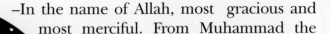

–In the name of Allah, most gracious and most merciful. From Muhammad the Messenger of Allah to Heraclius the Emperor of Byzantine. Peace be upon those who follow righteous guidance. I bid you to hear the divine call. Embrace Islam and attain salvation that Allah may double your reward. If not, you will pay the price for the sins of your subjects. "O followers of earlier revelation! Come unto that tenet which we and you hold in common: that we shall worship none but Allah, and that we shall not ascribe divinity to aught beside Him, and that we shall not take human beings for our lords beside God." And if they turn away, then say: "Bear witness that it is we who have surrendered ourselves unto Him."

Heraclius knew that Muhammad (saw) was a prophet based on what he had read and learned. He consulted the matter with his advisors. His intention was to embrace Islam. However, on seeing their reaction he did not. He treated the envoys well and sent them off with presents and gifts.

*On marching to Mecca, the Prophet saw a dog feeding its puppies. He immediately sent one of his companions and ordered that no one harm the animals.*

# The Conquest of Mecca and Returning Home

Two years passed since the signing of the Treaty of Hudaybiyyah. The pagans began to violate the treaty and they eventually revoked it completely. The Prophet then prepared and army of ten thousand soldiers and secretly moved towards Mecca. His objective was to capture the city without engaging in a battle or taking lives. Mecca was conquered without war.

Our beloved Prophet took the city of his birthplace and youth. He thanked Allah for this great conquest. He did not enter the town as an arrogant and successful commander but, rather with his head down and in praise of his Lord.

On reaching the hour of midday prayer, Bilal climbed onto the Ka'bah and made the call of adhan with his beautiful voice. On completing prayers, our Prophet turned to the people of the town and asked: "What are your thoughts, what do you think I will do to you now?"

Those who had tortured him and his companions in the past were helpless:

–We expect goodness. You are an honorable brother and the son of an honorable man.

The Prophet responded, "I say what Prophet Yusuf said. There is no humiliating this day. May Allah forgive you all. He is the most merciful of those who have mercy." and announced a general amnesty. He then cleared the idols from inside and around the Ka'bah and the Muslims remained in the town.

*The Prophet began distributing the booty after the battle of Hunayn. Even though they were not Muslims, various members of the Quraysh were given a larger share of the goods. Some of the Ansar said amongst themselves:*

*–Allah's messenger has turned back to his own people. During the battle we were his friends but, now his cousins and kinfolk are more important to him. We must talk to him and advise him to consider us more.*

*On hearing this, he gathered the Ansar and said:*

*–Are the worldly possessions that I have given these people in order to win the hearts of them so important to you? They return home with the goods of the world whereas, you return home with the messenger of Allah. If the entire world was to go in one direction and the Ansar in another, I would go with the Ansar.*

*On hearing this, the Ansar turned in remorse and cried.*

*–We are happy with giving our share to the messenger of Allah, they said.*

PART 7

# THEY ALL WEPT

## Farewell Hajj and Farewell Sermon

Hajj became an obligation after the conquest of Mecca. Our beloved Prophet journeyed to Mecca together with his family and companions in 632 to perform the Hajj (Pilgrimage).

After the conquest of Mecca, the number of people who embraced Islam grew rapidly. Our Prophet sent envoys to various regions in order to invite people to the religion. Within a short period of time, the entire Arabian Peninsula entered the fold of Islam.

Here, our Prophet made the historic speech. Over one hundred thousand people gathered to hear the message. In the speech, he mentioned that the God of mankind is one Allah, that all humans are of the same ancestor and that humans are equal. He

### From the Farewell Sermon

• All goods left in one's custody should be returned.

• The blood feuds of the Jahiliyyah are banned.

• Your spouses have rights over you as you have rights over them.

• Those who believe in Allah are brothers. It is not lawful to inappropriately take the goods of your brothers.

emphasized the rights of woman and reminded the gathering of the requirements of social harmony. Our Prophet once again reminded the whole mankind what the fundamental principals of the religion were.

# Farewell

On completing the Hajj (Pilgrimage), our beloved Prophet returned to Madinah. He was 63 years old. In those days, he would continually mention death and that he would die one day.

*• People! Your Lord is one. Your ancestor is one. Each of you have a common ancestor, Adam. And Adam was made of soil.*

*• The best person in the sight of Allah is he who fears him most. Neither of you are greater than each other. Greatness is in Taqwa (Fear and consciousness of Allah).*

He became ill and was unable to go to the mosque. He assigned Abu Bakr to lead the congregation of prayer. His condition deteriorated and he raised his right hand to the air pointing, "To be together with my Almighty Lord… Oh Allah, unite us in paradise." He had a smile on his face.

# The Departure: They All Cried

On hearing our Prophet's death, Abu Bakr came to the mosque immediately. Everyone was crying .He went directly to the Prophet's room. He removed the covers over his face and kissed his forehead:

–I sacrifice all I have for you O the Prophet of Allah. Your life was great, your death was great.

He came out of the room and then recited verse 144 of Surah Al-i Imran:

"And Muhammad is no more than an messenger; the messengers have already passed away before him; if then he dies or is killed, will you turn back upon your heels? And whoever turns back upon his heels, he will by no means do harm to Allah in the least and Allah will reward the grateful."

These words of Abu Bakr calmed all people who were in denial of the Prophet's death.

He was buried in the city of Madinah.

Our beloved Prophet was united with his Almighty

*The last revealed verse of the Holy Qur'an:*

*And guard yourselves against a day in which you shall be returned to Allah; then every soul shall be paid back in full what it has earned, and they shall not be dealt with unjustly.*

(Baqarah, 281)

Friend and Helper. He left us Muslims with two legacies, the word of Allah - the Holy Qur'an - and his exemplary life. He also gave the good news that whoever adheres to these two will attain success.

# Chronology of Prophet Muhammad's (saw) Life

| | |
|---|---|
| 570 | Abraha's army of the elephant attempts to destroy the Ka'bah |
| 570 | Death of our Prophet's father |
| 571 | Birth of the Prophet (April 20th) |
| 571-576 | Life with his foster mother Halima |
| 577 | Death of his mother Amina |
| 579 | Death of his grandfather Abdulmuttalib |
| 591 | Virtue Society membership |
| 596 | Marriage with Khadijah |
| 610 | First revelation received in the cave of Hira during Ramadan |
| 615-616 | Emigration to Abyssinia |
| 617-620 | Years of the boycott |
| 620 | Travel to Taif with Zayd |
| 620 | Miracles of the Isra and Miraj |
| 621 | First pact of Aqaba |
| 622 | Second pact of Aqaba |
| 622 | Emigration to Madinah |
| 622-624 | Construction of mosque and school, first call to prayer, announcement of brotherhood, the Madinah Agreement. |
| 624 | The Battle of Badr |
| 625 | The Battle of Uhud |
| 626 | The Biri Maun and Raji disasters |
| 626-627 | The Battle of Khandak |
| 628 | The Treaty of Hudaybiyyah |
| 630 | The Conquest of Mecca |
| 632 | The Farewell Sermon |
| 632 | The Prophet's death (June 8th) |